GREAT

CRITICAL THINKING

PUZZLES

Michael A. DiSpezio

Illustrated by Myron Miller

Sterling Publishing Co., Inc.   New York

Library of Congress Cataloging-in-Publication Data

Dispezio, Michael A.
    Great critical thinking puzzles / by Michael A. DiSpezio ;
illustrated by Myron Miller.
        p.   cm.
    Includes index.
    ISBN 0-8069-9725-7
    1. Puzzles. 2. Critical thinking. I. Miller, Myron, l948– .
II. Title.
GV1493.D557   1997
793.73—dc20   96–46532
                                                            CIP

    3   5   7   9   10   8   6   4   2

Published by Sterling Publishing Company, Inc.
387 Park Avenue South, New York, N.Y. 10016
© 1997 by Michael A. DiSpezio
Distributed in Canada by Sterling Publishing
c/o Canadian Manda Group, One Atlantic Avenue, Suite 105
Toronto, Ontario, Canada M6K 3E7
Distributed in Great Britain and Europe by Cassell PLC
Wellington House, 125 Strand, London WC2R 0BB, England
Distributed in Australia by Capricorn Link (Australia) Pty Ltd.
P.O. Box 6651, Baulkham Hills, Business Centre, NSW 2153,
Australia
Manufactured in the United States of America
All rights reserved

Sterling ISBN 0-8069-9725-7

CONTENTS

✦ ✦ ✦

Acknowledgments

Very few things are produced (or solved) in a vacuum. It is through the nurture, encouragement, playfulness, and caring of others that books such as *Great Critical Thinking Puzzles* are created.

With sincere gratitude, I appreciate the support and value that my family placed on education. Through the opportunities made available, I was (and am) able to purse my interests in creativity, teaching, performance, and science. Along the way, many individuals knowingly (and unknowingly) helped fine-tune my path. These people are friends and colleagues whose talents, skills, and capabilities have had a noted effect. They include Norman Levin, David Franz, William Harris, Ken Read, Steve Golubic, Peter Gascoyne, Edward O'Toole, Jonathan Elkus, Jonathan Larkin, Bob Higgins, Stewart (Buzzy) Hirsch, Karen Ostlund, Shirley Watt Ireton, Jocelyn Lofstrom, Bob Hall, Mike Kane, Warren Stone, Genie Stevens, Paul Mascott, Dennis Colella, Thomas Lineaweaver, Brian Shortsleeve, Doug Horton, my dedicated editor Hazel Chan, Myron Miller for his cartooning genius and puzzle-solving aptitude, and my friends, colleagues, and "extended family" in the Middle East and on Wilson Boulevard (NSTA).

Closer to home, I'd like to thank my son, Anthony, for being the best puzzle tester I've ever met.

INTRODUCTION

Hang on to your brains because here we go again!

In this follow-up adventure to *Critical Thinking Puzzles*, I present more of the best puzzles for stimulating your critical thinking skills. From mental paths to army ants, you'll encounter an assortment of challenges that are designed to pump up your brain power.

Psychologists and educators refer to critical thinking skills as a variety of higher-level thinking strategies that can be used to analyze, solve, and evaluate all sorts of things, such as facts, theories, statements, and, of course, puzzles. The array of brain-bending puzzles presented in this book should engage many of these skills.

You will have to uncover assumptions, solve by analogy, sequence events, generalize, and discover all sorts of patterns. You will also find yourself digging deeper into your brain to come up with some creative possibilities. Once generated, novel possibilities need to be analyzed in order to determine if they work.

As in my first book, there are old-time favorite puzzles with a new twist. For centuries, they have challenged and entertained people. But unbeknownst to the puzzled, these conundrums were also producing new thought channels that had been etched into the cells, chemicals, and electrical patterns of the brain.

Most of the puzzles here can be done with a pencil or pen. Others require simple items, such as loose change or matchsticks, that can be found around the house. But what they all need is for you to be creative and inventive in solving them.

So why wait? Just jump right in and you will be on your way to boosting your critical thinking skills again!

—*Michael*

THE PUZZLES

Brain Net

Your brain is an incredible piece of machinery. About the size of a squished softball, it contains billions of brain cells. These cells make more connections than all of the phones in the world. It's this huge network that produces your brain power! Want to feel the "brain net" in action?

Take a look at the drawing below. Your job is to figure out how many different paths can get you across from start to finish.

You can only move to the right. You can't go back. When you arrive at a "fork," take either the top or bottom route. Start counting.

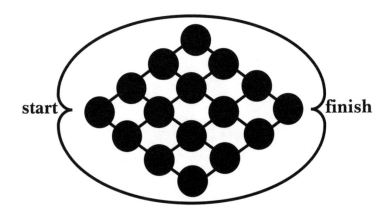

Answer on page 66.

Predicting Paths

✦ ✦ ✦

One of your brain's most powerful capabilities is the ability to think visually. When we think in this way, we construct a mind's eye image of a shape, scene, or concept. This image can be rotated, changed, moved, and analyzed. How good are you at visual thinking? Here's your first chance to find out.

Suppose we roll the wheel along the flat surface. Draw the shape that would be traced by the point within the wheel.

Now let's put the small wheel along the inner rim of a larger circle. What shape path would a point on the smaller wheel trace?

Finally, suppose the inner wheel remains stationary. What pattern would be traced out by a point on the larger rim as it rolls around (and remains in contact with) the inner wheel?

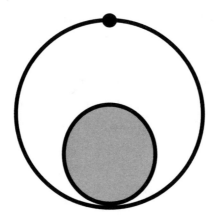

Answers on pages 66-67.

Who's That?

Look into a mirror and who do you see? You? Perhaps, but it's not the same you that everyone else sees. Its a right-left reversed image. The ear that appears on your left side is seen by others on your right side.

Suppose you want to see yourself exactly as others see you. How can you set up two small mirrors so that your reflection isn't reversed?

Answer on page 67.

Leftovers Again?

❖ ❖ ❖

Your brain is divided into two halves. The left half is more number-oriented, rational, and concrete. Your right half is more creative, playful, and artistic. To solve this next puzzle, you'll have to borrow a little from both sides of your brain.

In an art class, students are taught how to shape a 1 ounce bag of clay into a small statue. During this process, some clay remains unused (actually, it falls to the floor). For every five statues that are made, there is enough extra clay to make one more statue. Suppose a student is presented with 25 ounces of clay. What is the maximum number of statues he can sculpt?

Answer on pages 67-68.

Brownie Cut

✦ ✦ ✦

Now that art class is over, it's time for cooking class.

A chocolate brownie emerges from the oven. Karen cuts the square brownie in half. She then divides one of the halves into two smaller but equal parts.

Before she can eat the larger piece, two of her friends unexpectedly arrive. Karen wants everyone to have the same amount of dessert. In the fewest number of cuts, how can she produce three equal portions?

Answer on page 68.

Balancing Gold

✦ ✦ ✦

A gold bar balances with nine-tenths of 1 pound and nine-tenths of a similar gold bar. How much does each gold bar weigh?

Answer on page 68.

Thrifty Technique

✦ ✦ ✦

Don't put that balance away! You'll need it along with a few pounds of brain cells to help solve this next problem.

By the way, did you know that Albert Einstein's brain was "normal" in weight? For the most part, it resembled an ordinary brain. There was, however, a slight difference. He had extra "cleanup" cells (called neuroglial cells). These cells move around the brain to get rid of dead or injured nerve cells. Perhaps his "well swept" brain supercharged his intelligence?

You have nine gold coins. One of the coins is counterfeit and is filled with a lighter-than-gold substance. Using a balance, what strategy can you use to uncover the counterfeit coin?

To make things a little more difficult, you must identify the fake coin with only two uses of the balance.

Answer on pages 68-69.

Tricky Tide

✦ ✦ ✦

In the Bay of Fundy, the tides can vary in height by almost 50 feet. The bay in our puzzle has a tidal range of only 6 feet. A boat moors in the middle of this bay. A ladder hangs down from the deck of the boat and touches the flat sea surface. The rungs are 1 foot apart.

At low tide, ten rungs of the ladder are exposed. At high tide, the water level rises 6 feet. How many of the rungs will remain exposed?

Answer on page 69.

Breaking Up Is Hard to Do

How fast can you think? Faster than a speeding bullet? Faster than electricity? For most of us, thoughts race around our brains between 3 to 300 mph. Who knows, this puzzle may break your brain's speed record.

The square encloses a 4 × 4 grid. There are five different ways this grid can be divided into identical quarters. Each way uses a different shape. Can you uncover the layout of all five patterns?

Answer on page 69.

Disorder

Buildings crumble. Living things decompose. It's a scientific principle that things tend to go from order to disorder. The fancy name for this principle is entropy. There are, however, a few things that appear to go against this tendency. Crystals grow and become more complex. Living things take simple chemicals and build complex tissues.

This puzzle, however, uses entropy. Notice how neat and orderly the arrangement of numbers is. Now, let's play the entropy game and rearrange the numbers so that no two consecutive numbers touch each other. They cannot align side by side, up and down, or diagonally.

```
        ┌─────┐
        │  1  │
┌─────┬─────┬─────┐
│  2  │  3  │  4  │
├─────┼─────┼─────┤
│  5  │  6  │  7  │
└─────┼─────┼─────┘
        │  8  │
        └─────┘
```

Answer on page 69.

True or False?

Here's a totally different type of problem. This one is based on logic.

Two cultures of aliens live on the planet Trekia, the carpals and the tarsals. The carpals always lie. The tarsals always tell the truth.

A space traveler arrives on Trekia and meets a party of three aliens. She asks the aliens to which culture they belong. The first one murmurs something that is too soft to hear. The second replies, "It said it was a carpal." The third says to the second, "You are a liar!" From this information, figure out what culture the third alien belongs to.

Answer on page 70.

Pack Up Your Troubles

✦ ✦ ✦

A fragile item is to be shipped in a cardboard box. In order to prevent the item from hitting against the walls of the box, plastic foam cubes are used as "bumpers." There are ten of these cubes. How can you position them along the inner walls of the box so that there is an equal number of cubes along each wall?

Answer on page 70.

Don't Come Back This Way Again!

✦ ✦ ✦

The pitcher plant is a carnivorous plant that eats insects. An unfortunate insect walks into the pitcher plant's flower. When it tries to reverse direction, it can't. Tiny spines on the petals' surface face downward, which forces the insect to move in one direction—down.

Here's your chance not to go back. The shape below is made with one continuous line. Starting anywhere, can you complete the shape without lifting your pencil from the page? As you probably guessed, your path cannot cross over itself.

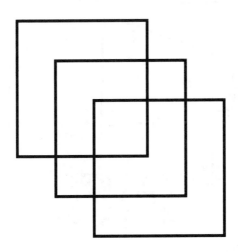

Answer on page 70.

Meet Me on the Edge

✦ ✦ ✦

Did you know that an ant can lift about fifty times its body weight? If you had that power, you'd be able to lift over 2 tons!

Suppose we position one of those powerful ants on a corner of a sugar cube. On the opposite corner, we position a fly. Suppose the two insects begin walking towards each other. If they can only walk along the edges of the cube (and never go backwards), what is the probability that their paths will cross?

Answer on page 71.

Only the Shadow Knows?

A medium-size jet has a wingspan of 120 feet. An albatross is a bird with a wingspan of about 12 feet. At what altitude would each object have to fly in order to cast shadows of equal size?

Answer on page 71.

More Shadow Stuff

At a certain time of day, a 25-foot telephone pole casts a 10-foot shadow. At that same time, how high would a tree have to be in order to cast a 25-foot shadow?

Answer on page 71.

Trip Times

Did you know that the speed record for cars is over 700 miles per hour? To attain this supersonic speed, the cars use rocket engines. They move so quickly that if the car body had wings, the vehicle would fly!

The car in our problem is much slower. In 1 hour, traveling at 30 mph, it climbs to the top of the hill. When the car reaches the top, the driver remembers that she left her field guide to mountain life back home. She immediately turns around and drives downhill at 60 mph. Assuming that she spent no time at the top, what was her average speed?

HINT: It is not 45 mph.

Answer on page 71.

Average Puzzle

How fast can you ride a bicycle? To get into the *Guinness Book of Records* for human-powered cycling, you'd need to ride faster than 60 mph.

An ordinary cyclist travels up and down a hill. Going up, she maintains a constant speed of 10 mph. It takes her 1 hour to get to the top. Assuming that the hill is symmetric, what speed must she maintain on the way going down if she wishes to average 20 mph? Before you bask in victory, the answer is not 30 mph.

Answer on page 72.

Palindrome

A palindrome is a word or number that reads the same backwards as it does forward. Numbers such as 606 and 4334 are palindromes.

While driving his car, Bob (so much of a palindrome lover that he changed his name from John to

Bob) observes that the odometer reading forms a palindrome. It displays the mileage 13,931.

Bob keeps driving. Two hours later, he looks at the odometer again and, to his surprise, it displays a different palindrome!

What is the most likely speed that Bob is traveling?

Answer on page 72.

Stacking Up

✦ ✦ ✦

Can you arrange these numbered blocks into three equal stacks so that the sum of the numbers displayed in each stack must be equal to any other stack.

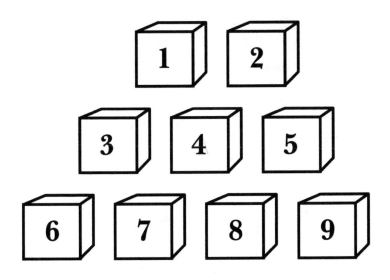

Answer on page 72.

Star Birth

Trace this octagon pattern onto a separate sheet of paper. Then decide how to divide this shape into eight identical triangles that can be arranged into a star. The star will have eight points and an octagon-shaped hole in its center. When you think you've come up with an answer, trace the pattern onto the octagon. Cut out the separate parts and reassemble them into a star.

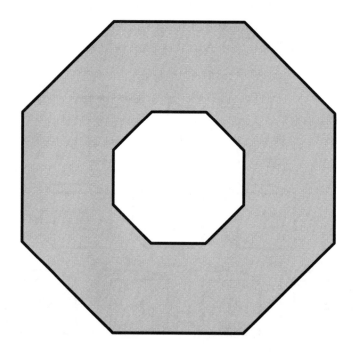

Answer on page 73.

Flip Flop

✦ ✦ ✦

Did you know that the ancient Egyptians believed that triangles had sacred qualities? This may have led to the superstition about walking under a ladder. When a ladder is placed against a wall, it forms a triangle. To walk through the triangle might provoke the wrath of the gods.

The triangle below is made up of ten disks. Can you move three of the disks to make the triangle point in the opposite direction?

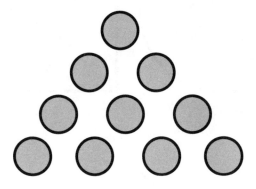

Answer on page 73.

Crossing Hands

✦ ✦ ✦

Picture in your mind a clock with a face and hands. Between the hours of 5 AM and 5 PM, how many times will the hour and minute hands cross each other?

Answer on page 73.

What's Next?

✦ ✦ ✦

Examine the figures below. Can you see what the pattern is and find out what the fourth figure in this series should look like?

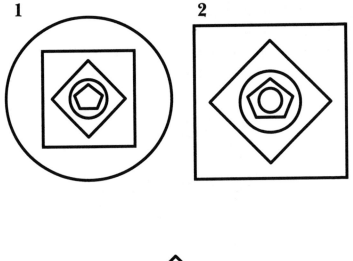

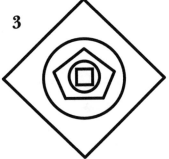

Answer on page 74.

Trying Triangles

♦ ♦ ♦

How many triangles can be found in this figure?

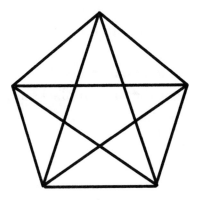

Answer on page 74.

Flipping Pairs

♦ ♦ ♦

Place three coins with their indicated side facing up as shown. In three moves, arrange the coins so that all three have the same side facing up. A move consists of flipping *two* coins over to their opposite side.

NOTE: Flipping the pair of outer coins three times doesn't count!

Answer on page 74.

Missing Blocks

Examine the figure of blocks below. Let's assume that the hidden blocks are all in place. How many additional blocks are needed to fill in the empty region to complete this cube?

Once you've made your guess, look at the pattern again. Assume that the hidden blocks are all in place. Now let's suppose that all of the blocks you can see are vaporized. How many blocks would be left behind?

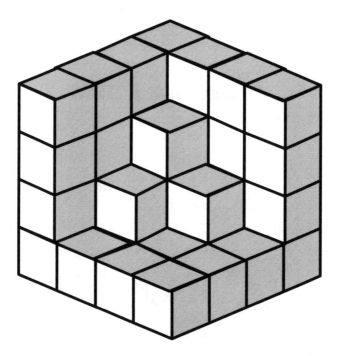

Answers on page 75.

Matchstick Memories

Years ago, matchsticks were made from small sections of wood. These common and inexpensive objects were perfect props for after-dinner or parlor room activities. Nowadays, toothpicks offer the same advantages. So get your picks together and arrange them in the three patterns shown below.

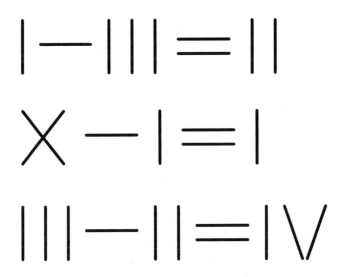

As you can see, each line of matchsticks forms an incorrect equation. The challenge is to make each one correct by changing the position of only one of the toothpicks in each row.

Answers on page 75.

Sum Circle

✦ ✦ ✦

Place the numbers one through six within the six smaller circles shown below. Each number must be used only once. The numbers must be placed so that the sum of the four numbers that fall on a circle's circumference is equal to the sum of the numbers on any other circle's circumference.

Think it's easy? Give it a try.

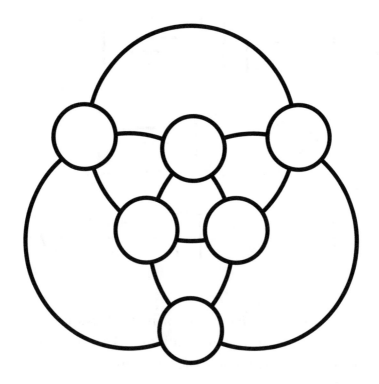

Answer on page 75.

Many Rivers to Cross

✦ ✦ ✦

Let's take a break from puzzles and go on a rowboat ride across the river. There are four adults who want to cross it. They come upon a boy and a girl playing in a rowboat. The boat can hold either two children or one adult. Can the adults succeed in crossing the river? If so, how?

Answer on page 76.

Train Travel

✦ ✦ ✦

A train travels at a constant rate of speed. It reaches a stretch of track that has fifteen poles. The poles are placed at an equal distance to each other. It takes the train 10 minutes to travel from the first pole to the tenth pole. How long will it take the train to reach the fifteenth pole?

Answer on page 76.

Miles Apart

✦ ✦ ✦

The distance from New York to Boston is 220 miles. Suppose a train leaves Boston for New York and travels at 65 mph. One hour later, a train leaves New York for Boston and travels at 55 mph. If we assume the tracks are straight paths and the trains maintain a constant speed, how far apart are the trains 1 hour before they meet?

Answer on page 76.

Passing Trains

✦ ✦ ✦

Coming from opposite directions, a freight train and a passenger train pass each other on parallel tracks. The passenger train travels at 60 mph. The freight train travels at 30 mph. A passenger observes that it takes 6 seconds to pass the freight train. How many feet long is the freight train?

HINT: There are 5,280 feet in a mile.

Answer on page 77.

Souped-Up Survey

✦ ✦ ✦

A survey agency reported their results in the local newspaper. The report states that exactly one hundred local lawyers were interviewed. Of the one hundred, seventy-five lawyers own BMWs, ninety-five lawyers own Volvos, and fifty lawyers own both a BMW and a Volvo.

Within a short time after the report, several lawyers argue that the survey results are incorrect. How can they tell?

Answer on page 77.

Toasty

✦ ✦ ✦

In order to make French toast, Ricardo must fry both sides of a bread slice for 30 seconds. His frying pan can only hold two slices of bread at once. How can he make three slices of French toast in only 1½ minutes instead of 2 minutes?

Answer on page 78.

Circle Game

Examine the pattern of circles below. Can you place the numbers one through nine in these circles so that the sum of the three circles connected vertically, horizontally, or diagonally is equal to fifteen?

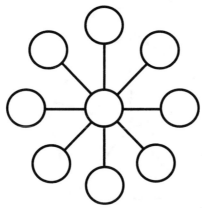

Answer on page 78.

A Fare Split

Michelle rents a car to take her to the airport in the morning and return her home that evening. Halfway to the airport, she picks up a friend who accompanies her to the airport. That night, she and her friend return back to Michelle's home. The total cost is $20.00. If the amount to be paid is to be split fairly, how much money should Michelle pay?

Answer on page 78.

Pentagon Parts

The pentagon below is divided into five equal parts. Suppose you color one or more parts gray. How many different and distinguishable patterns can you form? Each pattern must be unique and not be duplicated by simply rotating the pentagon.

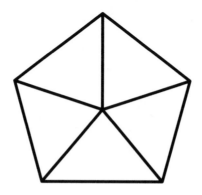

Answer on page 79.

Bagel for Five?

You and four friends have decided to split a bagel for breakfast. The five of you are not fussy about the size of the piece each will receive. In other words, all the pieces don't have to be the same size.

Using two perfectly straight cuts, is it possible to divide this bagel into five pieces?

Answer on page 79.

Coin Moves

Place twelve coins in the pattern shown below. Notice how they form the corners of six equal-sized squares. Can you remove three of the coins to have only three equal-sized squares remaining?

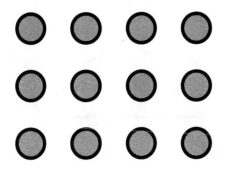

Answer on page 79.

Trapezoid Trap

✦ ✦ ✦

Divide the trapezoid below into four identical parts.

Answer on page 80.

A+ Test

✦ ✦ ✦

Here's a math challenge of a different sort. Trace these five shapes onto a sheet of stiff paper. Use a pair of scissors to carefully cut them out. Then assemble the shapes into a "plus" sign.

Answer on page 80.

Mis-Marked Music

✦ ✦ ✦

There are three boxes filled with audiocassette tapes. One box contains rap tapes, another contains jazz tapes, while the third contains both rap and jazz tapes. All three boxes have labels identifying the type of tapes within. The only problem is that all of the boxes are mislabeled.

By selecting only one box and listening to only one tape, how can you label all three boxes correctly?

Answer on page 80.

Measuring Mug

✦ ✦ ✦

Without the aid of any measuring device, how can you use a transparent 16-ounce mug to measure a volume of water that is exactly 8 ounces?

Answer on pages 80-81.

Coin Roll

✦ ✦ ✦

Two identical coins are positioned side by side. In your mind's eye, roll the coin on the left (Coin A) over the other coin (Coin B). When Coin A reaches the opposite side of Coin B, stop. In which direction will Coin A's head be facing?

Now, let's suppose that Coin A rolls completely around Coin B. If so, how many rotations does Coin A make around its own center?

Answers on page 81.

Painting on the Side

You are presented with several white cubes and a bucket of red paint. To make each of them different, you decide to paint one or more sides of each cube red. How many distinguishable cubes can you make with this painting method? Remember that any painted side must be painted completely to make it distinguishable from any other painted side.

Answer on page 81.

Magic Triangle

✦ ✦ ✦

Here's a magic triangle whose sides are formed by sets of four numbers. To solve the puzzle, place the numbers one through nine each in one of the circles. When you are finished, the sums of all three sides must be equal.

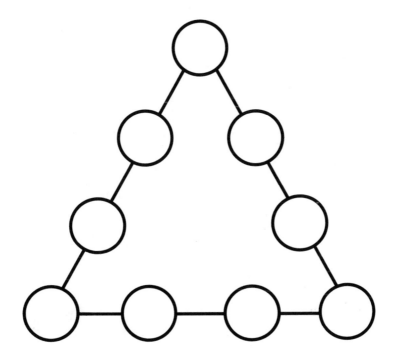

There are three different sums that can be used to reach the solution. Can you find all three?

Answers on page 82.

Patterns

The arrangement of numbers below represents a pattern. This pattern is a mathematical relationship between the numbers in each square, so don't look for things like spelling, days of the week, cryptograms, or codes. Can you uncover the pattern and fill in the question mark in the last square?

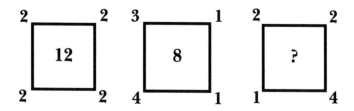

Answer on page 82.

Frog Jump

✦ ✦ ✦

A frog falls into a well that is 18 feet deep. Every day the frog jumps up a total distance of 6 feet. At night, as the frog grips the slimy well walls, it slips back down by 2 feet. At this rate, how many days will it take the frog to jump to the rim of the well?

Answer on page 82.

Army Ants

✦ ✦ ✦

Two small armies of ants meet head-on along a jungle path. Both armies would prefer to pass each other rather than fight. There is a small space along the side of the path. It is only large enough to hold one ant at a time. Is it possible for the armies to pass each other? If so, how?

Answer on page 83.

No Sweat

There are six players on a coed volleyball team. After an exhausting game, each girl drinks 4 cups of water. Each boy drinks 7 cups of water. The coach drinks 9 cups.

A total of 43 cups of water is consumed by everyone. How many boys and how many girls are on the team?

Answer on page 83.

Go Figure!

In a distant planet, there are four forms of life beings: zadohs, pugwigs, kahoots, and zingzags. All zadohs are pugwigs. Some pugwigs are kahoots. All kahoots are zingzags.

Which of the following statement(s) must then be true?

1. Some zadohs are zingzags.
2. Some kahoots are zadohs.
3. All kahoots are pugwigs.
4. Some zingzags are pugwigs.
5. All zingzags are zadohs.
6. Some zadohs are kahoots.

Answer on page 84.

Square Pattern

Suppose you have to paint all nine squares in the grid below using one of three colors: red, blue, or green. How many different patterns can you paint if each color must be represented in every row and every column? Each pattern must be unique. In other words, a new pattern can't be made by simply rotating the grid.

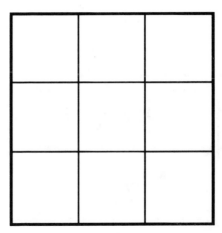

Answer on page 84.

Bouncing Ball

Did you know that when a ball strikes the ground, its shape distorts? This distortion stores the energy that powers its rebound. The more its shape changes, the higher the ball will bounce.

The ball in this puzzle rebounds to half the height from which it is dropped. Suppose it is dropped from a 1 meter height. What distance would the ball travel before it comes to rest?

Answer on pages 84-85.

Complete the Pattern

✦ ✦ ✦

Use the pattern below to determine the value for X and Y.

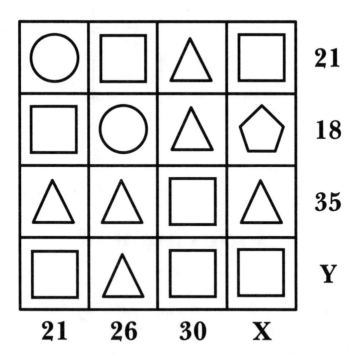

Answer on page 85.

Checkerboard

A full-size checkerboard has eight rows and eight columns that make up its sixty-four squares. By combining the patterns of these squares, you can put together another 140 squares. The pattern below is one-fourth the area of a full size checkerboard. What is the total number of squares that are found in this smaller pattern?

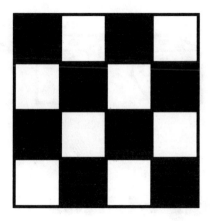

Answer on page 85.

Cutting Edge

Kristin wants to remodel her home. To save money, she decides to move a carpet from one hallway to another. The carpet currently fills a passage that is 3 × 12 feet. She wishes to cut the carpet into two sections that can be joined together to fit a long and narrow hallway that is 2 × 18 feet. What does her cut look like?

Answer on page 85.

The Die Is Cast

✦ ✦ ✦

Which die is unlike the other three?

Answer on pages 85-86.

Playing with Matches?

✦ ✦ ✦

Thirty-two soccer teams enter a statewide competition. The teams are paired randomly in each round. The winning team advances to the next round. Losers are eliminated. How many matches must be played in order to crown one winner?

Answer on page 86.

Competing Clicks

✦ ✦ ✦

Let the Mouse Click Competition Begin!

Emily can click a mouse ten times in 10 seconds. Buzzy can click a mouse twenty times in 20 seconds. Anthony can click a mouse five times in 5 seconds. Assume that the timing period begins with the first mouse click and ends with the final click. Which one of these computer users would be the first to complete forty clicks?

Answer on page 86.

Another Pattern

Here is another mathematical pattern that relates the four numbers of each triangle. Can you uncover the pattern and use it to complete the third triangle?

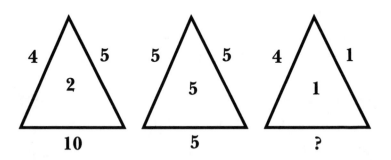

Answer on page 86.

Vive le Flag

The French tricolor flag is made up of three vertical stripes: red, white, and blue. Suppose you are given four different colors of fabric and asked to create a different flag using the same tricolor design. If no two adjacent stripes can be the same color, how many different combinations of color patterns are there?

HINT: Don't forget that the flag pattern can be flipped over!

Answer on page 87.

Pizza Cut

◆ ◆ ◆

Five people want to share a square pizza. The first person (who is really hungry) removes a quarter of the pie. When the others find out, they are annoyed and try to divide the remaining three-fourths into four equal and identically shaped slices. The cuts must be straight. How must they cut the remaining pizza in order to produce four identical slices?

Answer on page 87.

Slip Sliding

✦ ✦ ✦

For this challenge, you'll need to get seven coins. Place a coin on any of the star's eight points. Then slide the coin along one of the straight lines to its endpoint. Place a second coin on another point. Slide this one down to its endpoint. Continue in this manner until all seven coins have been placed.

NOTE: It can be done—but you'll need to develop a strategy.

Answer on page 87.

A, B, See?

Each letter stands for a different digit in each equation. Can you decode each one?

$$
\begin{array}{r}
AB \\
\times AB \\
\hline
ABB
\end{array}
\qquad
\begin{array}{r}
AA \\
+AA \\
\hline
BBC
\end{array}
\qquad
\begin{array}{r}
ABA \\
+BAB \\
\hline
BBBC
\end{array}
\qquad
\begin{array}{r}
ABA \\
+BAA \\
\hline
CDDD
\end{array}
$$

Answers on page 88.

Spare Change

Jonathan has a pocket full of coins. Yet he doesn't have the right combination of coins to make change for a nickel, dime, quarter, half dollar, or dollar.

What is the largest value of coins Jonathan can have in his pocket?

Answer on page 88.

Puzzling Prices

A puzzle book costs $5.00 plus one-half of its price. How much does the puzzle book cost?

HINT: It's more expensive than this book.

Answer on page 88.

Gum Drop

✦ ✦ ✦

In preparation for a party, Heather fills a large jar with gum drops. Before the party begins, Michael sees the gum drop jar. He (hoping that no one will realize) takes one-third of the drops. Soon after, Tanya takes one-third of the gum drops (she too hopes that no one will notice). Finally, Britt appears and, like the others, she takes one-third of the gum drops. If forty gum drops are left in the jar, how many did it originally contain?

Answer on page 88.

Go-Cart Crossing

Three go-cart tracks are built as shown. Each track forms a separate one-third of a mile loop. Three go-carts begin riding at the same time from the central point where all three tracks cross. One go-cart travels at 6 mph, another at 12 mph, and the third at 15 mph. How long will it take for all three go-carts to cross paths for the fifth time?

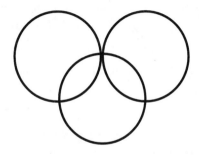

Answer on page 89.

Table Manners

Four couples enter a restaurant. How many ways can they be seated at a round table so that the men and women alternate and no husband and wife sit next to each other.

Answer on page 89.

Winning Slip

✦ ✦ ✦

A contest is fixed. Everyone knows it, including the contestants. One of the contestants, however, makes it to the final playoff level.

The master of ceremonies presents the following challenge: "This box contains two slips of paper. One slip has the word 'winner' printed on it, the other has the word 'loser.' Your task is to select the winning slip—without looking of course."

The contestant knows that this challenge is fixed. He realizes that both slips have the word 'loser.' How can he select one slip and win the challenge? By the way, the contestant can't declare this contest is a fraud or he'd lose his current winnings.

Answer on page 89.

Ancient Man

✦ ✦ ✦

An ancient Greek was said to have lived one-fourth of his life as a boy, one-fifth as a youth, one-third as a man, and spent the last 13 years as an elderly gent. How old was he when he died?

Answer on page 90.

Lights Out!

✦ ✦ ✦

The total output of electrical energy from your brain is only about 20 watts. That's not an avalanche of power (especially when you consider that most household light bulbs use five times that amount). Now try powering up with this problem.

Imagine that you can't sleep because you are kept awake by the flashing neon lights that shine through a square store window. The window measures 10 × 10 feet.

A friend assures you that he can cover up half the area of the window but still leave a square section that is 10 × 10 feet. This will then satisfy both you and the storekeeper. You think your friend has lost it. Has he?

Answer on page 90.

Pencil Puzzle

✦ ✦ ✦

Can you uncover the logic used to create this layout? If so, use that same logic to determine the letter for the question mark.

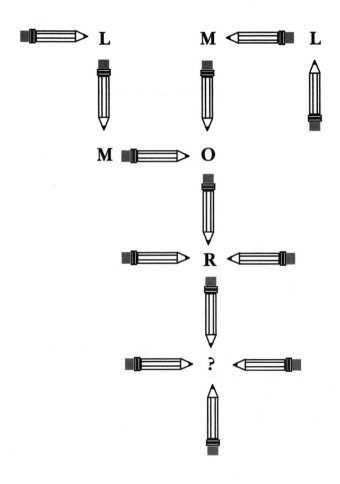

Answer on pages 90-91.

Sounds Logical?

It's the weekend! Saturdays and Sundays are the days that Sheila, Ramon, and Niko shop together for music. The CDs they purchase are either rock 'n' roll or jazz. When they visit the music store, each person will purchase one and only one CD. Here are the rules that govern their selections.

1. Either Sheila or Ramon will pick rock 'n' roll, but not both of them.

2. If Sheila picks rock 'n' roll, Niko picks jazz.

3. Niko and Ramon do not both pick jazz.

Which one of the three purchased a jazz CD on Saturday and a rock 'n' roll CD on Sunday?

Answer on page 91.

Triangular Tower

Suppose ten billiard balls are placed in the standard triangular rack. If additional billiard balls are placed on top of this pattern, some balls will roll into the gullies to form a smaller, stable triangle (forget about the balls which roll off the stack). If you add more layers, you'll eventually build a billiard ball pyramid. How many billiard balls and levels would the pyramid contain?

Answer on page 91.

Criss-Crossed

✦ ✦ ✦

Place six coins in the layout as shown below. Notice that this arrangement forms two columns. The horizontal column has four coins. The vertical column has three coins. Can you move only one coin to form two columns with each containing four coins?

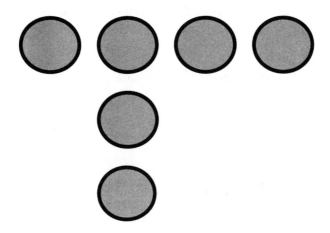

Answer on page 92.

Crystal Building

✦ ✦ ✦

Have you ever looked closely at a crystal? If so, you may have noticed that the crystal has flat sides and uniform angles. That's because a crystal is a repeating arrangement of tiny particles of matter. Often, a central particle is surrounded on all sides by other particles. Here's a puzzle that will help you visualize a crystal pattern.

Suppose you coat a tennis ball with glue. What is the maximum number of tennis balls that can attach directly to this sticky surface?

Answer on page 92

Testy Target

✦ ✦ ✦

Ten arrows are shot at the target below. One of them misses the target completely. The others all strike it. If the total sum of points is one hundred, in which part of the target did each arrow strike?

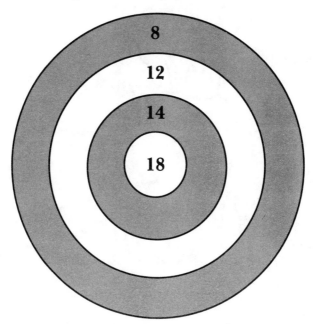

Answer on page 92.

Eighth Century Enigma

✦ ✦ ✦

Here's a puzzle that can be traced back to the eighth century. A man has a goat, a wolf, and a head of cabbage. He comes to a river and must bring these three things across to the other side. The boat can only take the man plus either the goat, wolf, or cabbage. There is another problem. If the cabbage is left with the goat, the goat will eat the cabbage. If the wolf is left with the goat, the goat will be devoured. How can he transport the wolf, goat, and cabbage to the other side?

Answer on page 93.

Planet Rotation

✦ ✦ ✦

Our planet spins counterclockwise on its axis. It also has a counterclockwise revolution around the sun. Suppose both motions now go clockwise. How would this affect the apparent direction of sunrise and sunset?

Answer on page 93.

Shuffle

✦ ✦ ✦

Pretend you have five cards: a ten, a jack, a queen, a king, and an ace. In your mind's eye, shuffle these five cards together and put the pile face down. If you were to select four cards, returning each card and reshuffling the deck after each pick, what kind of hand would you more likely draw: four Aces or a straight picked in sequence? Can you explain why?

Answer on page 93.

Some Exchange

✦ ✦ ✦

The first written puzzles appeared in ancient Egypt at about 1650 B.C. These puzzles were part of an 18½-foot scroll called the Rhind Papyrus. Times have changed since then, but many puzzles haven't. Just try these next ones.

Examine the two stacks of number blocks. If you exchange one block from one column with one block from the other, the number of their sums will be equal. Which blocks need to be exchanged?

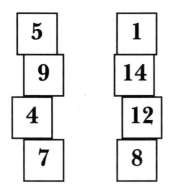

Now that you know how to balance two columns, you're ready to move up to three columns! By exchanging one block from each column, each of the three blocks' sums will be equal. Remember that all three columns must undergo only one exchange.

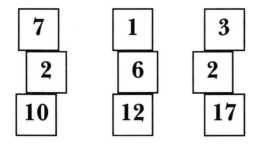

Answers on pages 93-94.

THE ANSWERS

Brain Net

Twenty routes. Although you can chart them all out, there is a less confusing way. Starting at the left, identify the number of routes that can get you to a circle. You can arrive at this number by adding the numbers found in the connecting circles to the left. Keep going until you get to the finish.

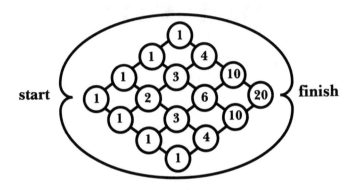

Predicting Paths

a.

b.

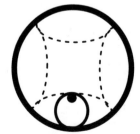

c.

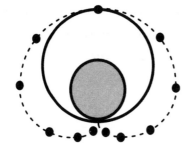

Who's That?

Position the mirrors so that they are arranged like an opened book. The right side of your face will reflect on the right side of the mirror. This image does not reflect back to that eye. Instead, it bounces to the other mirror. From there, the image is reflected back to the other eye.

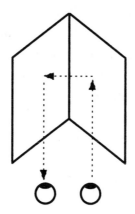

Leftovers Again?

Thirty-one statues. The 25 ounces are used directly to make twenty-five statues. During this process, 5 ounces of excess clay are produced. This extra clay is used to make five additional statues. While making these five additional statues, there is enough unused clay to make one more statue with one-fifth of the clay left over.

Brownie Cut

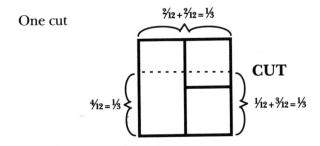

One cut

$\frac{2}{12} + \frac{2}{12} = \frac{1}{3}$

$\frac{4}{12} = \frac{1}{3}$

CUT

$\frac{1}{12} + \frac{3}{12} = \frac{1}{3}$

Balancing Gold

Nine pounds. Examine the objects on the right side of the balance. If we looked at the balance pan containing the two bars, we'd see that one-tenth of the gold bar is absent. In its place we have nine-tenths of a pound. From this we can infer that one-tenth of a gold bar weighs nine-tenths of a pound. Therefore, a complete gold bar would weigh ten times as much. $\frac{9}{10}$ pound $\times$ 10 = $\frac{90}{10}$, or 9 pounds.

Thrifty Technique

First, divide the coins into three groups of three. Then, balance any one group against another group. If the counterfeit is contained in either of the groups, the coins will not balance. If, however, they balance, the counterfeit coin must be in the third pile. Now that we have identified the pile with the counterfeit coin, remove one coin from the pile and balance the other two. The lighter coin will not balance. If the two coins do balance, the counterfeit coin is the one not selected.

Tricky Tide

Five rungs will still remain exposed. As the tide comes in, the boat will rise up.

Breaking Up Is Hard to Do

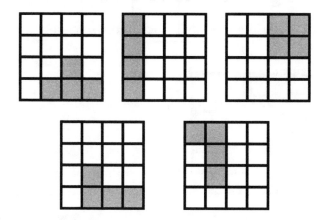

Disorder

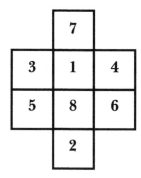

True or False?

Tarsal. To figure this one out, we need to look at each alien's response. If the first alien was a tarsal, it would identify itself as a tarsal. If it was a carpal, it would still identify itself as a tarsal. Either way, the mumbling alien would identify itself as a "tarsal." Therefore, the second alien had to be lying. The third alien truthfully identified the carpal, making him a truth-telling tarsal.

Pack Up Your Troubles

The "trick" is using the same block in the rows of two adjacent sides.

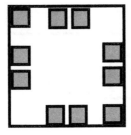

Don't Come Back This Way Again!

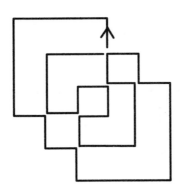

Meet Me on the Edge

One in six. The ant (or fly) can take any one of the six available routes. It doesn't matter.

Now, the other insect must select the "collision route" from its own six possible choices. Therefore, the odds are one in six.

Only the Shadow Knows?

They can never cast shadows of equal size.

Any difference in their altitude would be negligible compared to their distance to the sun. It's those 93,000,000 miles from our planet to the sun that affect the shadows' size much more than their puny distances apart.

More Shadow Stuff

At that time of day, the shadow is two-fifths of the object's height. If the tree's shadow (two-fifths of the unknown height) is 25 feet, then the height of the tree is 62½ feet.

Trip Times

Since it takes her 1 hour to reach the top (while traveling at 30 mph), the hill is a 30-mile route. Traveling at 60 mph, she'll cover that distance in only 30 minutes.

The average speed is the total distance/total time = 60 miles/1.5 hours or 40 mph.

Average Puzzle

There is no way that she can average 20 mph for the whole trip. Like the uphill path, the downhill path is only 10 miles. This distance is too short to achieve an average speed (for the whole trip) of 20 mph.

Consider this: If she completed her trip by traveling the downhill path at 600 mph, then her average speed would be the total distance divided by the total time, or 20 miles/61 minutes, or an average of about 19.6 mph.

By examining this equation, you'll see that there will be no way for her to decrease the denominator (time) below the 60 minutes she has already spent cycling up the hill.

Palindrome

55 mph. The next palindrome that the odometer can display is 14,041. To reach this value, Bob will have had to travel 110 miles. If it took him 2 hours to reach this point, his average speed will be 55 mph.

All other palindromes would have required too many miles to produce a logical speed. For example, the odometer's next palindrome is 14,141. From this, you can calculate an average speed of 105 mph—highly unlikely.

Stacking Up

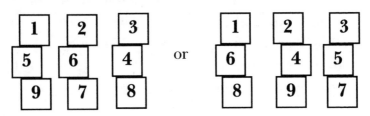

Star Birth

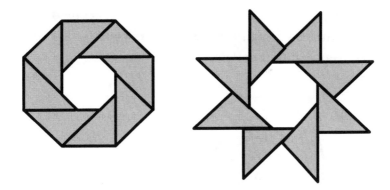

Flip Flop

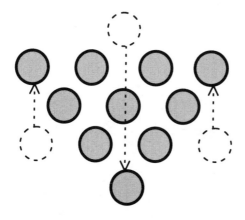

Crossing Hands

Eleven times. For each hour up until 11:00, the clock's hands will cross once. Between 11 AM and 1 PM, they'll only cross once (at noon). For each remaining hour between 1 PM and 5 PM, the clock's hands will cross once. That gives us a total of 6 + 1 + 4 = 11 times.

What's Next?

The sequence is based on the expanding geometric figures. After each figure reaches the outside perimeter, it starts again at the center.

Trying Triangles

Thirty-five triangles.

Flipping Pairs

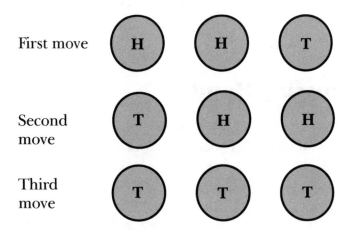

First move   H   H   T

Second move   T   H   H

Third move   T   T   T

Missing Blocks

a. Twenty-three blocks. None are missing from the bottom layer, six are missing from the second layer, eight are missing from the third layer, and nine are missing from the top layer.

b. Seventeen blocks. Eight are hidden in the bottom layer, six are hidden in the second layer, three are hidden in the third layer, and none are hidden in the top layer.

Matchstick Memories

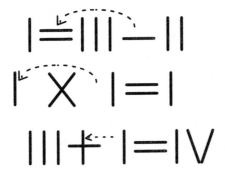

Sum Circle

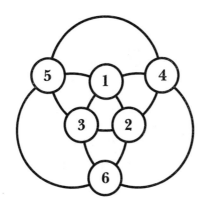

Many Rivers to Cross

First, the two children row to the far side. There, one gets out. The other child returns and gives the boat to an adult. The adult crosses the river. On the far side, the adult gets out and the child gets in the boat. The child brings the boat across the river and transports the other child back to the far side. This pattern continues until the four adults have crossed.

Train Travel

15 minutes and 32 seconds. This problem is not as simple as it may appear. The distance from pole one to pole ten is nine units. As stated, it takes the train 10 minutes to travel this distance. Therefore, it takes the train 1 minute and one-ninth (about 6.6 seconds) to travel each inter-pole distance.

From the first pole to the fifteenth pole is fourteen inter-pole distances. It should take 14 × 1 minute and 6.6 seconds, or 14 minutes and 92 seconds, or about 15 minutes and 32 seconds.

Miles Apart

120 miles. This problem is full of extra (and unneeded) information.

Think it backwards. One hour before they meet, one train is 65 miles away from the meeting point, while the other is 55 miles. Add the two distances together and you'll get 120 miles.

Passing Trains

792 feet. The length of the freight train can be calculated by knowing its relative passing speed and the time it took for it to move by. The passing speed is equal to the sum of both train speeds (60 mph +30 mph = 90 mph).

Here's where some conversion comes in. By dividing by sixty, we find that 90 mph is equal to 1.5 miles per minute. By dividing by sixty again, we find that this is equivalent to 0.025 miles per second.

The freight train takes 6 seconds to pass. Therefore, its length is 0.15 miles. To change this into feet, multiply 0.15 by the number of feet in a miles (5,280).

Souped-Up Survey

The numbers do not add up correctly. The agency stated that only one hundred people were interviewed. Yet, according to a logical breakdown of the results, they received 120 responses. You can see by making a diagram of the data.

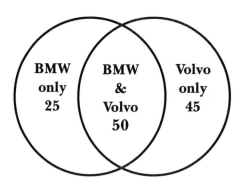

Toasty

Fry one side of two slices for 30 seconds. Flip one slice over and replace the other slice with a fresh slice of bread. At the end of 1 minute, remove the completely fried bread. Return the unfried side of the previous slice to the pan and flip the other slice over for 30 seconds.

Circle Game

When added together, the numbers at the opposite ends of this sequence equal ten (1 + 9, 2 + 8, etc.). By placing a five in the middle circle, we ensure that all the sums must equal fifteen (10 + 5).

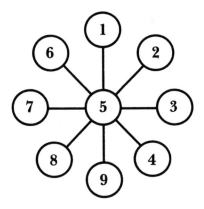

A Fare Split

$12.50. One-fourth of the total round trip fare ($5.00) was taken by Michelle alone. Three-fourths of the round trip was shared (half of $15.00). Therefore, Michelle should pay $5.00 + $7.50 or $12.50.

Pentagon Parts

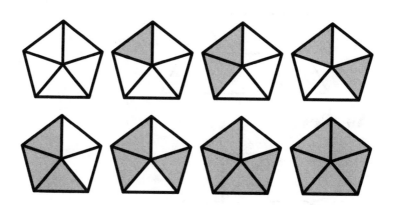

Bagel for Five?

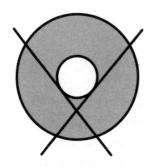

Coin Moves

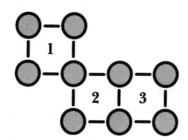

Trapezoid Trap

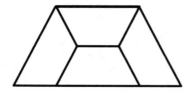

A+ Test

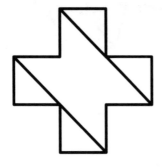

Mis-Marked Music

Select the box labeled "Rap & Jazz." Listen to one tape. If the marble is jazz, then you must have the box full of jazz cassettes. (Remember that since all the boxes are mislabeled, this box could not contain the mix of rap and jazz.) Likewise, if the tape is rap, you have selected the all-rap box. Since all three names are mismatched, then just switch the names of the other two boxes to correctly identify the contents of all boxes.

Measuring Mug

Fill the mug about two-thirds full of water. Then tilt it so that water pours off. When the level of water reaches the same height as the uplifted mug bottom, the vessel is then half full.

Coin Roll

a. The same direction—to the left.

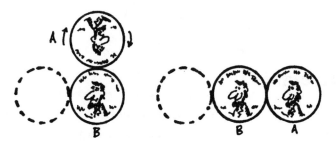

b. Two.

Painting on the Side

Ten ways. 1 = all sides white, 1 = one red face, 1 = two adjacent red faces, 1 = two opposite sides red faces, 1 = three sides red (in line), 1 = three faces red (in right-hand and left-hand L-shape design), 1 = four faces red (in line), 1 = four faces red (two pairs of two in line), 1 = five red faces, 1 = all faces red.

Magic Triangle

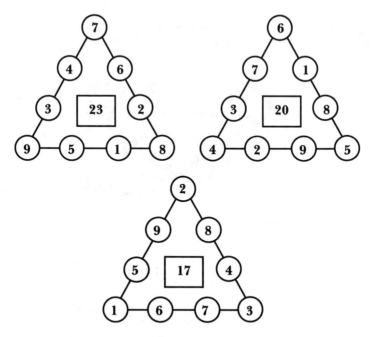

Patterns

Fourteen. Add the upper left number, lower left number, and lower right number together. Then multiply this sum by the number in the upper right corner. The product is in the center of the square.

Frog Jump

Four days. During the first day, the frog jumps up 6 feet and at night slides down 2 feet. The frog begins day two at a height of 4 feet, jumps to 10 feet, but slides back to 8 feet. On day three, the frog jumps to 14 feet, but slides back to 12 feet. On day four, the frog jumps to 18 feet and leaves the well.

Army Ants

Yes. Here's how.

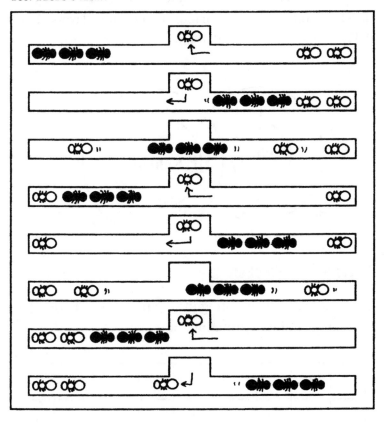

No Sweat

Five girls and two boys. First, subtract the coach's 9 cups from the total amount. Therefore, the boys and the girls together drank 34 cups. The winning combination is five girls (who together drink 20 cups) and two boys (who together drink 14 cups). 20 + 14 = 34 cups.

Go Figure!

Statement 4. The confusing relationship may best be understood by putting the information in a graphic layout. From the drawing, you can see that only statement 4 is true.

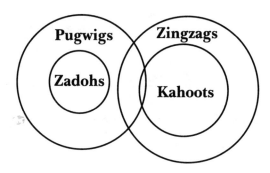

Square Pattern

There are only three distinguishing patterns. All other patterns are obtained by rotating the square.

r	g	b
b	r	g
g	b	r

b	g	r
r	b	g
g	r	b

g	r	b
b	g	r
r	b	g

Bouncing Ball

Approximately 3 meters. The first fall is 1 meter. It rebounds to ½ meter, than falls ½ meter. So now we're at 2 meters. Then the ball goes up and down ¼ meter, then

⅛ meter, then ¹⁄₁₆ meter, and so on. It continues this pattern until it comes to rest (theoretically it would keep going, but in the real world it stops). If we were to add all of these distances up, we'd get: 1 + ½ + ½ + ¼ + ¼ + ⅛ + ⅛ + ¹⁄₁₆ + ¹⁄₁₆ +... = ~3 meters.

Complete the Pattern

X = 22; Y = 25. Each circle equals 1, each square equals 5, each triangle equals 10, and the pentagon equals 2. The numbers represent the sums of the values in each row or column.

Checkerboard

Thirty squares.

Cutting Edge

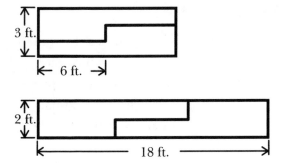

The Die Is Cast

Although all four dice have the same relative orientation of spots, the three spots on the last die tilt from the lower left corner to the upper right corner.

When the other dice are rotated onto this position, their three spots tilt from the upper left to the lower right corner.

Playing with Matches?

Thirty-one matches. If one winner is to be found in thirty-two teams, then thirty-one teams must lose. Since each team can only lose once, the thirty-one losses result from thirty-one matches.

Competing Clicks

Anthony. The actual period is 1 second less than the time given. Emily completes ten clicks in 9 seconds. Buzzy completes twenty clicks in 19 seconds. Anthony completes five clicks in 4 seconds. This gives us the approximate rates: Emily = 1.1 clicks/second, Buzzy = 1.05 clicks/second, Anthony = 1.25 clicks/second.

Another Pattern

Four. The number in the center of each triangle results from dividing the product of the top two sides by the bottom side.

Vive le Flag

Twenty-four combinations. If both of the outside stripes are the same color, you'll have twelve possible combinations ($4 \times 3 = 12$).

If all three stripes are a different color, you'll have twenty-four possible combinations ($4 \times 3 \times 2 = 24$). However, these twenty-four flags are made up of twelve mirror-image pairs. Just rotate the mirror image one-half turn and you'll produce the other flag. This decreases the stripe combinations to only twelve.

Now let's add the two sets of possible combinations: $12 + 12 = 24$ different color patterns.

Pizza Cut

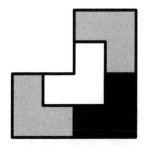

Slip Sliding

You'll get blocked if you don't place the coins in a specific order. Each coin must come to rest on the spot where the previous coin began its journey. Only in this manner can you then place all seven coins.

A, B, See?

10	55	919	545
×10	+55	+191	+455
100	110	1110	1000

Spare Change

$1.19. Jonathan has four pennies, four dimes, one quarter, one half dollar. Added together, they amount to $1.19.

Puzzling Prices

Ten dollars. The trick is not getting fooled into thinking that the book is five dollars.

If the book is "p," then $5 + ½p = p.

$5 = ½p.

$10 = p.

Gum Drop

135 gum drops. If forty gum drops are left in the jar, the forty must represent two-thirds of the gum drops that were available when Britt appeared.

Therefore, the total number of gum drops before Britt took her share was sixty. Working with the same logic, you can figure out that before Tanya took her share of thirty, the jar had ninety gum drops. Before Michael took his share of forty-five, it had 135 gum drops.

Go-Cart Crossing

33.3 minutes. To travel 1 mile, go-cart A takes ⅙ of an hour, go-cart B takes 1/12 of an hour, and go-cart C takes 1/15 of an hour. To travel one loop distance (⅓ of a mile), it would take each 1/18, 1/36, and 1/45 of an hour, respectively. All three would meet at ⅑ of an hour intervals. For five meetings to occur, five ⅑-hour periods must pass. 5 × ⅑ = 5/9 of an hour, or about 33.3 minutes.

Table Manners

Two ways. White = female. Black = male.

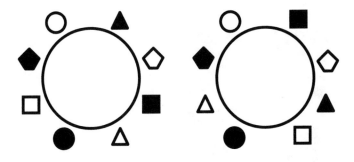

Winning Slip

The contestant picks one of the slips. The slip is placed out of view (possibly eaten). The contestant then asks the MC to read the slip that was not selected. That MC's slip has the word "loser." When the audience hears "loser," they logically conclude that the contestant must have picked the winning slip.

Ancient Man

60 years old. If his whole life is "X years," then:

His boyhood years = ¼X

His youth = ⅕X

His adulthood = ⅓X

His elder years = 13

¼X + ⅕X + ⅓X + 13 = X

X = 60

Lights Out!

He covers the window as shown here, which meets both conditions.

Pencil Puzzle

V. The layout is based on the sequence of letters found in the alphabet. The "twist" is produced by the extra pencil points aimed at certain letters. Each pencil point can be replaced by the words "advance one step."

Look at the letter L (either one). The L progresses to M. The M, however, does not advance to an N because two M pencil points converge on this next space. The letter then advances one extra step, resulting in an O.

With the same logic, the O leads to an R (advance three steps). The R leads to a V (advance four steps).

Sounds Logical?

Niko. If Sheila picks rock 'n' roll, then according to (1) Ramon must pick jazz and according to (2) Niko must also pick jazz. These selections contradict (3). This rules Sheila out.

If Ramon picks jazz, then according to (1) Sheila must pick rock 'n' roll and the same contradictions surface.

The only person who can select either jazz or rock 'n' roll without any contradictions is Niko.

Triangular Tower

Twenty balls arranged in four levels.

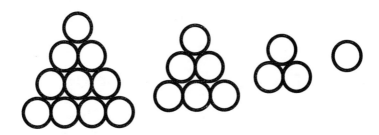

Criss-Crossed

Place one coin on top of the corner coin.

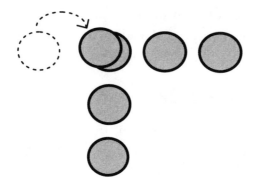

Crystal Building

Twelve tennis balls. Place six in a circle around the middle of the ball. Place three on top and three on the bottom.

 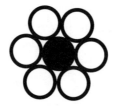

Testy Target

Two arrows struck the 8 region (16 points) and seven of them struck the 12 region (84 points). Total: 16 + 84 = 100 points.

Eighth Century Enigma

On his first trip, the man brings the goat over (leaving the cabbage and wolf behind). On his second trip, he brings over the cabbage. When he lands on the other side, however, he takes the goat back in his boat. When he returns, he drops off the goat and takes the wolf. He transports the wolf across the river and leaves it with the cabbage. He returns once more to ferry over the goat.

Planet Rotation

The sun would now appear to rise in the west and set in the east. This change is caused by the switch in rotation spin. The switch in revolution does not affect the direction of the apparent sunrise or sunset.

Shuffle

The straight is more probable. To select the four of a kind, you need to select "one card out of five cards" four times: $\frac{1}{5} \times \frac{1}{5} \times \frac{1}{5} \times \frac{1}{5}$, or 1 out of 625.

For the straight, the first card can be any card. Then, you'll need to select "one card out of five cards" three times: $\frac{1}{5} \times \frac{1}{5} \times \frac{1}{5}$, or 1 out of 125—a better probability.

Some Exchange

a. 14 and 9. The sum of all eight numbers is sixty. Each column must have a sum equal to half that, or thirty. To arrive at thirty, you need to lessen one column by five and increase the other by the same amount. This is accomplished by exchanging a 14 for a 9.

b. 2, 1, and 3. As with the previous problem, you can add all nine numbers together, then divide that sum by three. The result is twenty:

7	2	1
3	6	2
10	12	17
20	20	20

INDEX

Page key: puzzle, *answer*.

About the Author

Michael DiSpezio has always had a fondness for integrating learning with creativity, critical thinking, and performance. After tiring of "counting hairs on copepods," Michael traded the marine science laboratory for the classroom. Over the years, he has taught physics, chemistry, mathematics, and rock 'n' roll musical theater. During his classroom years, Michael co-authored a chemistry book, which launched his writing career.

To date, Michael is the author of *Critical Thinking Puzzles* (Sterling) as well as eighteen science textbooks, a producer of several educational videos, and a creator of hundreds of supplementary products and science education articles. His most recent science education project was authoring *The Science of HIV*, a teaching package published by the National Association of Science Teachers.

Michael's expertise in both video and science education has resulted in several trips to train counterparts in the Middle East. When he isn't presenting workshops for science teachers, Michael is at home writing, creating, and puzzle solving.